UNDERSTANDING GOD'S WORD WORKBOOK

UNDERSTANDING GOD'S WORD WORKBOOK

An Introduction to
Interpreting the Bible

JON NIELSON

WHEATON, ILLINOIS

Understanding God's Word Workbook: An Introduction to Interpreting the Bible
© 2025 by Jon Nielson
Published by Crossway
        1300 Crescent Street
        Wheaton, Illinois 60187

All rights reserved. No part of this publication may be reproduced, stored in a retrieval system, or transmitted in any form by any means, electronic, mechanical, photocopy, recording, or otherwise, without the prior permission of the publisher, except as provided for by USA copyright law. Crossway® is a registered trademark in the United States of America.

Cover design: Zach DeYoung

First printing 2025

Printed in Colombia

Unless otherwise indicated, Scripture quotations are from the ESV® Bible (The Holy Bible, English Standard Version®), © 2001 by Crossway, a publishing ministry of Good News Publishers. Used by permission. All rights reserved. The ESV text may not be quoted in any publication made available to the public by a Creative Commons license. The ESV may not be translated in whole or in part into any other language.

Trade paperback ISBN: 978-1-4335-8747-4

Crossway is a publishing ministry of Good News Publishers.

NP			33	32	31	30	29	28	27	26	25
14	13	12	11	10	9	8	7	6	5	4	3	2	1

CONTENTS

Introduction *vii*

1 Basics of Bible Study *1*

2 The Context Tool *5*

3 The Courtroom Tool *19*

4 The Crux Tool *35*

5 The Construction Tool *51*

6 The Clarity Tool *67*

7 The Cross Tool *83*

INTRODUCTION

If you've ever been asked to teach the Bible, perhaps in a Sunday school or small-group context, you've probably felt the weight of some of these questions: Am I getting it *right*? Is *this* the main point of the text? Am I applying this passage *correctly* to God's people today? We want to be sure we're understanding God's word properly so that we can apply it faithfully to our lives as God intends.

All of these situations and struggles have to do with basic *biblical hermeneutics*—the process of understanding, interpreting, and applying the Bible. To help you learn to practice hermeneutics properly, *Understanding God's Word* gives you six basic hermeneutical "tools" that you can put to use as you read the Bible on your own, study it in small groups, or perhaps even teach it in certain settings. These tools include:

1. The *context* tool, which will help you notice and apply the historical, literary, and canonical context of the biblical passage you are studying.

2. The *courtroom* tool, which will remind you to commit to say neither more nor less than what Scripture says.

3. The *crux* tool, by which you'll make sure that you are studying any given biblical passage in light of the main theme of the book in which it is contained.

4. The *construction* tool, which will help you discern the structure and shape that the author has intentionally given to the passage.

INTRODUCTION

5. The *clarity* tool, by which you'll seek to leave behind your personal perspectives and agendas, allowing the biblical text to speak for itself.

6. The *cross* tool, which will help you always study the Bible in light of its climax: the person and work of Jesus Christ, the Savior and Lord.

I believe that if you use these tools faithfully and consistently, they will help you interpret the Bible accurately and apply it well.

To get the most out of this workbook, I encourage you to work through it as you read the book (and the biblical passages) carefully and thoroughly. Answer the questions fully and thoughtfully; the harder you work, the more you'll get out of this study.

I hope that *Understanding God's Word* will help you do just what the title suggests—better understand the Bible—so that you can benefit from and live by its timeless truths.

Chapter 1

BASICS OF BIBLE STUDY

Before we begin looking at the six hermeneutical tools that we'll unpack in the following chapters, it will be helpful to consider some foundational principles about the Bible and think about some habits we need to develop in order to study it successfully.

FOUNDATIONAL PRINCIPLES

Review pages 1–2 in *Understanding God's Word*

We study the Bible with confidence that it is God's inspired word—and is therefore powerful, inerrant, consistent, and unified. We need to commit to studying it faithfully and carefully, and applying it correctly; this is the discipline of biblical hermeneutics.

Answer the following questions briefly:

1. What truths about the Bible should encourage you as you study it? How can you expect God to act and work in the lives and hearts of his people as they study his word?

CHAPTER 1

Respond to the following questions in more depth:

1. Why should you have confidence in your study of God's word? What truths about the Bible should remind you of the importance of reading it, studying it, and actively seeking to apply it to your life as you follow Jesus?

SIX HABITS FOR SUCCESSFUL BIBLE STUDY

Review pages 4–7 in *Understanding God's Word*

It is good for you to cultivate these six habits in your Bible study. These habits map out a plan and approach for thoroughly and carefully studying any passage of Scripture, with proper attention to the details of the text, its context, its connection to Jesus Christ, and its faithful call for believers in Jesus today.

Answer the following questions briefly:

1. Why are these six habits helpful as a plan for Bible study? In your study of any given passage, what might they help you capture that you might otherwise miss?

Respond to the following questions in more depth:

1. How might these six habits be helpful as you consider a consistent and thorough approach to studying a specific passage in the Bible? How have you gotten lost or distracted in small-group Bible studies in the past—and how might this approach prevent that?

RECAP

The Bible is God's inspired, authoritative, inerrant, sufficient, and powerful word to us. As his people, we don't just hear Scripture once—we study it, learn it, meditate on it, and give ourselves to understanding it more deeply and applying it more faithfully. Therefore, it is good for us to remember what the Bible is and also to develop practical tools for continually knowing it more and more deeply. Ultimately, the discipline of Bible study demonstrates our love for God, who graciously gave us his word to guide our lives and our relationship with him.

SO WHAT?

As you conclude this chapter, jot down brief answers to the following application questions:

1. Why might it be practically helpful for us as we study the Bible to remember some of the core doctrines about the Bible? How might the doctrine of the Bible's inspiration, for example, shape the way you seek to intentionally apply Scripture (and prayerfully respond to God as you do so)?

CHAPTER 1

2. What are some ways you might already be thinking about changing your approach to Bible study (either on your own or in a small-group setting) based on what you've read in this first chapter?

Chapter 2

THE CONTEXT TOOL

Finding the right context of a Bible verse or passage is vitally important in order to make correct interpretations and applications. When you apply the context tool, you will begin to see the way that it can guard and protect you against false interpretations of the Bible, leading you to both interpret and apply God's word in the way that he intends.

UNDERSTANDING THIS TOOL

Review pages 9–13 in *Understanding God's Word*

We need to study, understand, and apply every text of Scripture in light of its historical, literary, and canonical context. When we fail to do this, we risk missing the main point and thus applying Scripture incorrectly.

As you prepare to dig deeper into the context tool, answer the following questions briefly:

1. Has another person ever taken something you said out of context? Explain what happened. Why was this confusing or frustrating?

CHAPTER 2

2. Can you think of any ways that you have seen a Bible verse or passage taken out of context in church, a Bible study, or a conversation? Did you notice it at the time?

3. What are some ways that you can make sure that you correctly understand the context of Bible passages in your study?

Respond to the following question in more depth:

1. Describe some dangers that you think might come from taking the Bible out of context. How might taking passages out of context actually distort our view of God, his work, his character, or his actions?

THE CONTEXT TOOL

PROBLEMS AVOIDED WITH THIS TOOL

Review pages 14–15 in *Understanding God's Word*

Ignoring the context of a Bible passage can lead to false interpretations, missed main points, and other problems.

Answer the following questions briefly:

1. What are some ways that you have seen people abuse or mishandle the Bible?

2. Can you think of any examples from history when people claimed that the Bible backed up their actions or beliefs even though it really did not?

3. What is so serious and harmful about claiming that the Bible says something when it really does not?

Respond to the following questions in more depth:

CHAPTER 2

1. If someone asked you to evaluate the context of a Bible verse, what would you do first? What steps would you go through?

BENEFITS RECEIVED WITH THIS TOOL

Review pages 15–17 in *Understanding God's Word*

Paying careful attention to the historical, literary, and canonical context of a passage of Scripture helps us hear God's word as the original authors intended and as the original audience heard it. Doing so also helps us find the real relevance of the Bible.

Answer the following questions briefly:

1. Discuss people's desire for the Bible to have relevance for them. If God is the Creator of all things and the Savior of all who believe in his Son, then what is the most relevant way to study his word?

2. What benefits do you enjoy when you understand the intended meaning of a passage of Scripture—the meaning that both the human authors and God intended the passage to have?

THE CONTEXT TOOL

Respond to the following questions in more depth:

1. Describe a time when you studied, read, or learned about part of the Bible and felt confident that you understood the right interpretation of that passage. How did you feel? How did you want to respond? Why were you so confident in the correct meaning of that part of the Bible?

APPLYING THIS TOOL

Let's now see how the context tool can help us correctly interpret several passages.

Jeremiah 29:11

Review pages 17–19 in *Understanding God's Word*

Jeremiah 29:11, when ripped from its context, can seem to be a promise of *earthly* health, wealth, and success for God's people. However, given the passage's context—the exile of God's people in Babylon—it is actually a promise of *ultimate* joy and victory for God's faithful children despite earthly trial, pain, and suffering.

Answer the following questions briefly:

CHAPTER 2

1. What is the most important reason, in your opinion, to put the context tool to work in the study of Scripture?

2. Why is it important not only to find the right interpretation of Bible passages, but also to consider some ways that people might interpret them incorrectly?

3. As you practice using the context tool, what do you hope to learn about faithfully studying God's word?

Respond to the following questions in more depth:

1. What are some ways that Jeremiah 29:11 could be taken out of context to mean something that it really does not mean? Explain how, and why, this might happen.

2. Considering the wider context (historical, literary, and canonical), what is the right interpretation of God's promise to his people in Jeremiah 29:11?

Philippians 4:13

Review pages 19–21 in *Understanding God's Word*

If the context is not considered, Philippians 4:13 can be understood as a promise of accomplishment through the power of Christ. In its context, though, it is about contentment in Christ—whatever the circumstances.

Answer the following questions briefly:

1. In your opinion, what motivates some people to rip verses from their context? Explain how some of these motivations might not be bad, but might still lead to false interpretations of God's word.

CHAPTER 2

2. What are some things that you have learned to watch for in a Bible passage in order to not miss the context?

Respond to the following questions in more depth:

1. When you read Philippians 4:13 on its own, what kinds of interpretations and applications do you come to? Give specific examples.

2. When you read Philippians 4:10–13, how is the way you read verse 13 affected? What issues of context impact the way that we should apply this well-known verse?

THE CONTEXT TOOL

Revelation 3:20

Review pages 21–23 in *Understanding God's Word*

Revelation 3:20 can seem to be about a gentle Jesus addressing unbelievers, but when we read it in its context, we see that it is actually a strong rebuke to professing believers in the church.

Answer the following questions briefly:

1. Give an example of how the tone of a comment can be completely determined by its context—either in a conversation or a situation. Have you ever seen someone's tone completely misinterpreted so that it changed the apparent meaning of the person's words?

2. What are some important issues related to the historical context of the book of Revelation that should not be missed when we seek to interpret it properly?

Respond to the following questions in more depth:

1. Write a summary of an interpretation of Revelation 3:20 that does not take the context into account. How would Jesus be presented in such an interpretation? What would the tone of this verse seem to be? How does the surrounding context correct that interpretation?

CHAPTER 2

1 Corinthians 13

Review pages 23–25 in *Understanding God's Word*

First Corinthians 13:1–7, when read on its own, can sound like a gentle, sweet poem about love. In its context in Paul's letter, though, we find that it is a rebuke to the Corinthian Christians, who are not acting in a loving way toward one another at all.

Answer the following questions briefly:

1. Why has tone been such an important part of our context discussion in this and the previous biblical example? Why is it important to grasp the tone of a passage as we seek to apply it to our lives as Christians?

2. What are your initial impressions of 1 Corinthians 13? Where have you heard this chapter read or taught? How was it read?

Respond to the following question in more depth:

THE CONTEXT TOOL

1. What are some hints that you see in 1 Corinthians 13 that remind you that this passage is related to other parts of Paul's letter? How do these hints give you a sense of Paul's tone in this part of the letter?

Genesis 39

Review pages 25–27 in *Understanding God's Word*

Genesis 39 seems to come out of nowhere—and is often read without any reference to the chapter right before it. But that context is important. Chapter 39 shows Joseph fleeing from sexual temptation far from the land of promise and yet experiencing the presence of God—in contrast with chapter 38, which shows Joseph's brother Judah living in the land of promise but giving in to sexual sin and falling out of favor with God.

Answer the following questions briefly:

1. Why is it so important to find the true emphasis of the biblical author in any given passage, account, or story?

CHAPTER 2

2. What is the danger of missing the true emphasis of a part of Scripture? How might missing the true emphasis affect the way we apply God's word to our lives?

Respond to the following questions in more depth:

1. Genesis 37 is about Joseph. Genesis 38 is about Judah. Genesis 39 returns to the story of Joseph. What might the author be trying to show us by jumping around like this? How does the organization of this story (the context) show us the author's emphasis in this part of the book of Genesis?

RECAP

This chapter has introduced you to the first of six tools for your study of the Bible—the context tool. This tool helps you understand a passage as the author meant it to be read and as the original audience actually read it. You learned about three main kinds of context: historical, literary, and canonical.

SO WHAT?

As you conclude this chapter, jot down brief answers to the following application questions:

THE CONTEXT TOOL

1. What do you think is the most valuable lesson that you have learned during this chapter on the context tool?

2. Why is it so important for us to remember that the Bible was written by real human men, under the inspiration of the Holy Spirit, who lived in specific places at specific periods in history? What might we miss in our Bible interpretation if we fail to acknowledge this?

3. How can you make sure that you put this tool to work as you study, apply, and even teach the Bible? How will you be sure to remember the importance of context?

Respond to the following question in more depth:

1. In a few sentences, make an argument for the importance of the context tool. Summarize what the tool helps us do, the mistakes it helps people avoid, and its value for Bible interpretation and application.

CHAPTER 2

Chapter 3

THE COURTROOM TOOL

When we study, interpret, and apply God's word, we need to commit to say neither more nor less than what the Bible says. The courtroom tool helps us do that.

UNDERSTANDING THIS TOOL

Review pages 30–31 in *Understanding God's Word*

In every American courtroom, a witness who takes the stand during a trial is asked, "Do you swear to tell the truth, the whole truth, and nothing but the truth?" When that question is answered affirmatively, the witness can then be examined and the trial can continue.

That commitment is the main idea behind the hermeneutical tool that we are learning about and putting to work in this chapter: the courtroom tool. When it comes to interpreting and applying the Bible, we are called as Christians to give the whole truth of God's word—and nothing but that truth!

Answer the following questions briefly:

1. What are some ways that you can imagine people failing to speak or believe the whole truth about the Bible? Where or when have you seen such a failure?

CHAPTER 3

2. What are some ways that you can imagine people saying more than the truth that the Bible teaches—that is, adding things to God's word? Where or when have you seen this?

3. How do you think the courtroom tool will be valuable to you in your study of the Bible?

Respond to the following question in more depth:

1. Describe the thought process you would go through and the steps that you would take to make sure that you understand, speak, and apply "the truth, the whole truth, and nothing but the truth" of a specific passage in the Bible.

PROBLEMS AVOIDED WITH THIS TOOL

Review pages 31–33 in *Understanding God's Word*

When we apply the courtroom tool, we avoid problems such as legalism and spiritual pride that can result from false interpretations and misleading applications.

Answer the following questions briefly:

1. What might motivate a person to try to make the Bible say *more* than it actually says?

2. What might motivate a person to try to make the Bible say *less* than it actually says?

3. Why is it so hard to say "the truth, the whole truth, and nothing but the truth" when it comes to Scripture?

Respond to the following question in more depth:

CHAPTER 3

1. Write out some instances when you personally might be tempted to say either more or less than what the Bible says. How can you fight these temptations?

BENEFITS RECEIVED WITH THIS TOOL

Review pages 33–34 in *Understanding God's Word*

Applying the courtroom tool faithfully helps us maintain the careful balance and tension of Scripture—that is, it keeps us on the "line" of the truth of God's word.

Answer the following questions briefly:

1. Why is it so important to maintain the tension and the balance of Scripture? How is it beneficial to your faith to remember that God is both holy and gracious? That we are both saved by grace and called to active obedience?

2. Was it helpful to see the distinction between legalism and license, and the dangers that can come from both mistakes? How can recognizing the dangers of both legalism and license lead us toward a right understanding of both Scripture and our Christian walk?

Respond to the following question in more depth:

1. Describe some of the greatest benefits of faithfully seeking to understand the truth, the whole truth, and nothing but the truth of God's word. If you do this well, how will it help you in your walk with Jesus Christ?

APPLYING THIS TOOL

Let's now see how the courtroom tool can help us correctly interpret several passages.

Genesis 3:1–7

Review pages 34–36 in *Understanding God's Word*

Genesis 3:1–7 tells us about the first "battle" over God's word in the Bible, with Satan saying less than what God had spoken, and Eve responding by saying more than what he had said. The tragic result is disobedience to God's word, and sin enters the world.

Answer the following questions briefly:

CHAPTER 3

1. What do you think is your personal tendency toward God's word—to *add* to it or to *subtract* from it?

2. Why are these tendencies equally dangerous?

Respond to the following questions in more depth:

1. How does Eve fail to speak "nothing but the truth" of God's word in this passage? How does the serpent fail to speak "the whole truth" about God's word in this passage?

2. What would it have looked like for Adam and Eve to speak God's whole truth and nothing but that truth?

Mark 7:1–13

Review pages 36–38 in *Understanding God's Word*

In Mark 7:1–13, Jesus notes that the Pharisees are saying more than God's word, adding their traditions to the clear teaching of Scripture. Jesus explains to them that by doing this they have actually ended up subtracting from God's word, making it "void" (v. 13).

Answer the following questions briefly:

1. What are some noble purposes or good intentions that might tempt someone to add to God's word?

2. What are some ways that we might see the Pharisees' error with regard to God's word played out in church or religious life today? What rules or rituals have you seen added to the Bible?

CHAPTER 3

Respond to the following questions in more depth:

1. How can a legalistic tendency begin to twist our understanding of the character of God? In what ways does adding things to God's word—and then trying to enforce those additions on other people—affect our view of others and our relationships with them?

Matthew 5:27–30

Review pages 38–39 in *Understanding God's Word*

As we apply Matthew 5:27–30, we can say more than what God's word commands by taking Jesus's command in a wooden, literal way; but we can also say less than what it commands by failing to apply Jesus's powerful and urgent call to put sin to death.

Answer the following questions briefly:

1. From what you have seen from the accounts of Eve and the Pharisees, what would you say is on the line as we respond to God's word and apply it to our lives? Why is it so important to hear and apply God's word correctly?

THE COURTROOM TOOL

2. Are there ways that you have felt especially challenged so far in this chapter about how you interact with God's word? How are you growing in your understanding of the right response to the Bible?

Respond to the following questions in more depth:

1. As you think about Matthew 5:27–30, which is focused on the sin of lust, what are some ways that you can imagine people wanting to say *less* than what this passage is teaching? What are some ways that people might want to use this passage to say *more* than what Jesus is saying? What approach makes best use of the courtroom tool?

1 John 1:5–10

Review pages 40–41 in *Understanding God's Word*

First John 1:5–10 can be used—depending on the section one emphasizes the most—to teach either sinless perfectionism or sinful license. We need to allow the tension of God's word to hold sway in our interpretation and application of this passage. Believers in Christ must not continue in unrepentant sin, yet forgiveness and grace are always available to Christians who do sin.

CHAPTER 3

Answer the following questions briefly:

1. How does a good understanding of Jesus's substitutionary death for sins on the cross help you apply 1 John 1:5–10 faithfully? In other words, why is the gospel very important as you apply the courtroom tool to that passage? How should the clear biblical call for Christians to pursue obedience and holiness shape our understanding of this passage?

2. Is using the courtroom tool beginning to come naturally to you? What is still confusing to you? What are you still hoping to learn about putting this tool to work in your study of the Bible?

Respond to the following question in more depth:

1. As you consider this passage from 1 John, how would you summarize the different perspectives on sin in the lives of believers that could result from the reading of this passage?

Matthew 24:32–44

Review pages 41–43 in *Understanding God's Word*

As we study Jesus's teaching about the end of the world and the day of judgment in Matthew 24:32–44, we must be careful not to say more than what God's word says (making specific predictions about timing, etc.), but also not to say less than what it says (denying that Jesus will return and that there will be a final day of judgment for which we must be ready).

Answer the following questions briefly:

1. How is reading the Bible with balance different from reading it with compromise? How is recognizing a certain tension between two truths in the Bible different from failing to make strong statements about biblical truth?

2. As you think about the second coming of Jesus Christ, in what ways do you think you need to adjust your thinking? Do you think very often about his coming to judge the world?

Respond to the following questions in more depth:

CHAPTER 3

1. How might some people say or do more or less than what the Bible teaches as they await the return of Christ to judge the world? What leads some people to try to figure out the precise time of his coming? How do some people fail to obey Jesus in their preparation and readiness?

Matthew 25:6–13

Review pages 43–44 in *Understanding God's Word*

Jesus's words about the poor in Matthew 25:6–13 remind us that Christians can tend to say more or less than what the Bible says about our call to serve and generously help those in need. Yes, Christians are called to give generously to the poor and help those in need. No, the call to help with tangible needs in the world should never overshadow the call to proclaim the gospel and invite people to place their faith in Jesus Christ.

Answer the following questions briefly:

1. What are some different perspectives about poverty among Christians? What are the reasons for the disagreements?

2. What are some ways that people might say *more* than what the Bible says about a Christian approach to poverty?

THE COURTROOM TOOL

3. What are some ways that people might say *less* than what the Bible says about a Christian approach to poverty?

Respond to the following question in more depth:

1. How should the person and example of Jesus Christ affect our attitude toward poverty in this world? What point is Jesus making to his disciples in this account from Matthew's Gospel?

RECAP

The purpose of the courtroom tool is to help you, like a good witness in a courtroom, to stay focused on speaking the truth, the whole truth, and nothing but the truth—specifically, the truth about God's word. Far too often, people end up saying or teaching

CHAPTER 3

more or less than what the Bible says. Faithful students of the Bible must have a balanced interpretation of it, holding certain truths with the right tension.

▼ SO WHAT?

As you conclude this chapter, jot down brief answers to the following application questions:

1. What are some of the most important lessons you have learned as we have discussed and applied the courtroom tool in this chapter?

2. What are some mistakes in Bible interpretation and application that this tool can protect us from?

3. Why is it important for Christians to use this tool as they study God's word?

Respond to the following question in more depth:

32

THE COURTROOM TOOL

1. How would you explain the courtroom tool to a person who is just beginning to study the Bible? Do this as clearly as you can, using simple and straightforward language.

CHAPTER 4

THE CRUX TOOL

When we talked about six habits for successful Bible study in chapter 1, we saw that one of those habits is "Identify 'core' terms." This habit can help you get closer to the "crux"—the main point, big idea, or central theme—of a passage from the Bible. Every biblical passage has a main point that the biblical author is trying to get across, and the same is true for whole books of the Bible. It's very important for us to find the main points of the biblical books—and that's where the crux tool comes in.

UNDERSTANDING THIS TOOL

Review pages 48–49 in *Understanding God's Word*

The crux tool reminds us that in order to find the main point and main application of any given biblical text, it is important to understand the overall theme of the entire book in which that passage is located. By using certain hints (the book's purpose statement, themes that recur at the beginning and ending, and repetition of words, phrases, and ideas), we can discover the crux of what biblical authors are trying to communicate to us as they write.

Answer the following questions briefly:

1. Have you ever read a book—a novel, perhaps—and wondered what the main point of it was? What books come to mind as you answer this question?

35

CHAPTER 4

2. Why is it important to know the main point—or the big idea—of a whole book as you read and study it?

3. If someone asked you to find the main point or main theme of a book in the Bible, how would you do so?

Respond to the following questions in more depth:

1. If you were writing a book, what are some ways that you would help your reader know your main point? Would you state it very openly and obviously? Would you weave it into your story? Would you keep it hidden from the reader until the very end of the story?

PROBLEMS AVOIDED WITH THIS TOOL

Review pages 49–50 in *Understanding God's Word*

Using the crux tool effectively helps students of the Bible avoid faulty interpretations, as well as applications that may be off base in terms of the overall message and theme of a biblical book. It reminds us to read and study passages as parts of biblical books, which is the way God has given his word to us.

Answer the following questions briefly:

1. Talk about a time when you got "lost" in the middle of your study in a book (any book—it does not have to be a book of the Bible). Why did you get lost? What were you missing? How did this experience make you feel?

2. Why is it important, in your study of a book, to find your way to a big idea that the book focuses on? How might that help keep you focused in your reading?

Respond to the following questions in more depth:

1. What are some of the main problems of failing to use the crux tool well in our study of a book in the Bible? How could ignoring this tool lead to frustration

CHAPTER 4

and confusion? How might this prevent you from understanding and applying the Bible well?

BENEFITS RECEIVED WITH THIS TOOL

Review pages 50–51 in *Understanding God's Word*

One of the chief benefits of using the crux tool is that it helps us come to understand the biblical author's main point for the biblical book as a whole. This helps us identify the book's main theme, to which we can then tether our study of smaller chunks of Scripture within that biblical book.

Answer the following questions briefly:

1. In addition to understanding the main point of a biblical book as a whole, what do you think some of the benefits of using this tool well might be? How might this tool help you in Bible study or teaching throughout a particular book?

2. Have you ever used this tool before in any way? If so, how? If not, do you think this has kept you from grasping the main point of books in the Bible?

Respond to the following questions in more depth:

1. Discuss some of the ways that knowing the big picture of a story, play, or movie helps you understand the individual parts, chapters, or scenes. Can you think of specific examples where this has happened for you?

APPLYING THIS TOOL

Let's now see how the crux tool can help us correctly interpret several passages.

The Book of Jude

Review pages 51–53 in *Understanding God's Word*

By paying careful attention to the purpose statement of Jude—and looking carefully at its beginning and ending—we can begin to find our way to the crux of this biblical book, which helps us understand it and apply it faithfully to our lives today.

Answer the following questions briefly:

CHAPTER 4

1. Does there seem to be a purpose statement in this letter? If so, what is that statement?

2. Does Jude repeat any words or themes throughout his letter? If so, why are these important?

3. Are there any similar words used in the beginning and end of this letter?

Respond to the following question in more depth:

1. How might all of the hints that you have observed lead you to the crux of this book? In what ways might this crux guide your study of the book of Jude? How might it guide the way you apply the book to your life as a follower of Jesus today?

The Gospel of John

Review pages 53–54 in *Understanding God's Word*

John's purpose statement in John 20:30–31 gives us a very good idea of the crux of this Gospel—and we see themes from the purpose statement repeated very intentionally throughout the book.

Answer the following questions briefly:

1. From what you already know about the Gospel of John, what do you think that the crux might be?

2. If you do not have time to read an entire book of the Bible, what are some shortcuts that you might take in order to begin finding your way to the big idea of that book?

Respond to the following questions in more depth:

CHAPTER 4

1. What are some elements of John's purpose statement (John 20:30–31) that you should expect to find in the overall crux of the book? What does John tell you about his intentional focus as he writes his Gospel?

The Gospel of Luke

Review pages 54–56 in *Understanding God's Word*

Luke gives us a purpose statement right at the beginning of his Gospel; his words help us understand the crux of this Gospel.

Answer the following questions briefly:

1. Take a moment to review the hints for finding the crux of a biblical book that we discussed in the "Understanding This Tool" section of chapter 4 in the book *Understanding God's Word*. What were the other two hints that we learned about in addition to the purpose statement? How might they show up in the Gospel of Luke?

2. John's purpose statement for his Gospel does not show up until chapter 20, whereas Luke's appears at the outset of his Gospel. Where might we normally expect to find a purpose statement? Why is this?

42

Respond to the following question in more depth:

1. Put forward your best formation of a crux for the Gospel of Luke, based on Luke 1:1–4. Try to back it up from other specific passages in the Gospel of Luke (some are referenced in the *Understanding God's Word* book).

The Gospel of Matthew

Review pages 57–58 in *Understanding God's Word*

The Gospel of Matthew has some big repeated ideas and themes that we can trace throughout the book and use to land on the crux of Matthew's account.

Answer the following questions briefly:

1. From what you already know about the four Gospels, how would you expect Matthew's focus or big idea to be different from both Luke's and John's?

CHAPTER 4

2. Why is it good to acknowledge that different Gospels can have different themes, even if we firmly believe that they are all about Jesus Christ—his life, death, and resurrection?

Respond to the following questions in more depth (referring to Matt. 1:1–17; 7:28–29; and 28:16–20):

1. What common theme (or themes) do you see in the three passages referenced above? How might that theme (or those themes) help you find your way to the crux of the book of Matthew? How would you summarize the crux of the book?

The Book of Romans

Review pages 58–60 in *Understanding God's Word*

Romans has themes that Paul references at both the beginning and end of the book; these themes lead us to his crux in this epistle.

Answer the following questions briefly:

THE CRUX TOOL

1. What do you know about the book of Romans? What is your general impression of this book?

2. Have you ever read or studied Romans before? If not, why not? If yes, what do you think might be the crux of this book?

3. When studying a biblical epistle (letter) like Romans, what are some good hints to look for when trying to discover its crux?

Respond to the following question in more depth (referring to Rom. 1:1–7; 3:21–26; and 16:25–27):

1. From the passages that you just read from the book of Romans, what elements do you think need to be included in the crux for this book? (You do not have to state

CHAPTER 4

an exact crux, but explain what you think needs to be a part of that main point or big idea for the book.)

The Book of Leviticus

Review pages 60–61 in *Understanding God's Word*

The book of Leviticus has recurring themes, phrases, and foci that lead us to understand the crux of the book.

Answer the following questions briefly:

1. In the biblical books we have studied briefly, what have you found to be the most helpful hint for finding the crux of these books? Have you discovered any other helpful hints for finding the crux?

2. Among the books that we have studied, which has been the easiest (in your opinion) for which to find the crux?

3. What aspects of the use of the crux tool are still challenging for you?

Respond to the following question in more depth (referring to Lev. 4:22–26; 15:31; 16:1–5; 19:1; and 19:37):

1. From the verses and passages in Leviticus referenced above, how would you begin forming a crux for the book? Think about the main themes that keep coming up. Try to put a good statement of the crux into one concise sentence.

RECAP

The crux tool is designed to help you find your way to the main point or big idea of an entire book in the Bible. We need to have a good grasp of the book's overarching point in order to understand the points of the individual parts. The crux tool can help you do that—and can serve you well as you study smaller passages within any book.

CHAPTER 4

▼ SO WHAT?

As you conclude this chapter, jot down brief answers to the following application questions:

1. What has been most helpful to you as you have learned about the crux tool? How will you put this tool to work in your future study of the Bible?

2. If you were going to begin studying the book of Joshua, what would you do first in order to find the crux of the book? What hints would you look for?

3. What would you still like to learn about the study of books of the Bible?

Respond to the following question in more depth:

1. Describe the crux tool as if you are trying to explain it to someone who has never heard of it. What is this tool? What is its purpose? How is it used?

THE CRUX TOOL

Chapter 5

THE CONSTRUCTION TOOL

The human authors of Scripture were inspired to write by God's Holy Spirit, but they wrote with careful attention to organization and structure. However, we often do not notice the structure of the biblical passages that we study. We simply read them and ask general questions—or make general comments—about them, or we focus on the impressions or feelings that these passages give us. When we study this way, failing to pay attention to the structure of the passages we are focusing on, we run the risk of making incorrect interpretations and applications. The construction tool can help us avoid this danger.

UNDERSTANDING THIS TOOL

Review page 65 in *Understanding God's Word*

Utilizing the construction tool in our study of Scripture enables us to see the shape of a given biblical passage (the way the biblical author has put it together) so that we can see what he intends as the main point—and main application—for God's people.

Answer the following questions briefly:

1. Have you ever read or studied a passage in the Bible that seemed random or confusing because you did not understand how the author was organizing

CHAPTER 5

his thoughts? Why would it be hard to interpret and apply a passage in that situation?

2. What problems in Bible study can be avoided when the structure of a Bible passage is clear and obvious?

Respond to the following questions in more depth:

1. Explain why a well-organized speech is easier to listen to—and interpret and apply—than a random spewing of words that does not have any organization. How does structure help us understand? How can structure and organization be a key to finding meaning in many different parts of life?

THE CONSTRUCTION TOOL

PROBLEMS AVOIDED WITH THIS TOOL

Review pages 66–67 in *Understanding God's Word*

The construction tool helps us avoid such problems as misplaced emphasis in our study of biblical passages; the assumption that the biblical authors wrote random thoughts; or literary abuse. When we discern the way the author shaped and formed the passage, we guard ourselves against missing his purpose or confusing his meaning.

Answer the following questions briefly:

1. When you were taught to write papers in school, what was the general approach you were instructed to use? How do you craft an email in order to help your reader understand the main point of your communication and avoid any confusion?

2. Why is it important to understand the biblical authors as *writers* who sought to give literary shape to what they wrote (as opposed to merely dictating truths and messages)?

3. Are you sometimes tempted to hone in on a key word that jumps out at you from a biblical passage, but which may or may not be tied to the main point of

53

CHAPTER 5

the text? In what ways might the construction tool help you guard against this tendency?

Respond to the following question in more depth:

1. What might it communicate to us about God if the Bible came to us as random, disconnected thoughts without clear organization? What do we learn about God's character and communication as we see the way the biblical authors carefully and thoughtfully crafted their words under the inspiration of the Holy Spirit?

BENEFITS RECEIVED WITH THIS TOOL

Review pages 67–68 in *Understanding God's Word*

The construction tool helps you see how a passage in Scripture (even a verse—or an entire book) is put together. It reminds you to pay attention to biblical structure. God inspired the human authors of Scripture, but they still wrote with literary intentionality, beauty, and organization.

Answer the following questions briefly:

THE CONSTRUCTION TOOL

1. Think about a time when you heard a very well-organized speech or read a very well-structured book. How did good "construction" help you understand and apply what was being said or taught?

2. What are some benefits, in your opinion, that can come from using the construction tool as you study passages from the Bible?

Respond to the following question in more depth:

1. From what you have learned so far, how would you summarize the importance of finding the construction of a passage in Scripture? How can doing so help you with the passage's meaning? How can this help you with interpretation and application of the passage?

CHAPTER 5

APPLYING THIS TOOL

Let's now see how the construction tool can help us correctly interpret several passages.

Psalm 19

Review pages 68–70 in *Understanding God's Word*

Psalm 19 is organized into three clear sections, which help us to see what the biblical author wants us to grasp about God's world, God's word, and the right response to the holy and glorious God.

Answer the following questions briefly:

1. Review some of the ways that we learned to find the structure of a passage in the Bible. As you read a psalm from the Bible, what hints should you be looking for to show you the way that the psalm is organized?

2. How can the structure of Psalm 19 lead you toward the right application? How will you determine that you have found that application?

Respond to the following questions in more depth:

THE CONSTRUCTION TOOL

1. What seem to be the main sections of Psalm 19? What hints help you see that these are the three main sections? What is the main point of each of the three sections of this psalm?

Luke 15

Review pages 70–72 in *Understanding God's Word*

Luke 15 is a carefully structured passage of Scripture, designed by Luke (and the Holy Spirit) to make a specific point. The shape of the entire chapter shows us the emphasis of the author.

Answer the following questions briefly:

1. Why are we sometimes tempted to skip the construction tool in our study of the Bible? Why is it sometimes difficult to put this tool to work? What kind of work does it require?

2. How might the structure of a Gospel be different from that of a psalm? What hints of construction should we expect to find in a Gospel account?

57

CHAPTER 5

Respond to the following questions in more depth:

1. Summarize the shape of Luke 15: How did Luke construct it? Then explain how this structure helps you understand what Luke (and Jesus) is trying to emphasize through this passage. To what main point is he directing the attention of his readers?

Philippians 2:5–11

Review pages 72–74 in *Understanding God's Word*

Philippians 2:5–11 has a very clear literary shape, which we must discern in order to see the truths that the passage teaches us about Jesus—and the example that Christians are called to follow.

Answer the following questions briefly:

1. Discuss how a biblical author can actually communicate something through the way in which he structures his message.

THE CONSTRUCTION TOOL

2. Have you ever read or studied a poem that had a shape that was part of its meaning and point? If so, what was it? What message was it teaching?

Respond to the following questions in more depth:

1. How does Philippians 2:5–11 begin, and what does that tell you about Paul's focus in these verses?

2. What is the general shape or direction of verses 6–8? What is the general shape or direction of verses 9–11?

CHAPTER 5

3. How does the structure of this passage lead you to an understanding and application of its main point?

Genesis 11:1–9

Review pages 74–76 in *Understanding God's Word*

Genesis 11:1–9 is a passage in the shape of a *chiasm*. That means there are echoes of the beginning at the end of the passage, and a central climactic point in the middle. It's good to look for chiastic structure in the Bible, as it is used quite often.

Answer the following questions briefly:

1. What are some important lessons that you have learned so far about the construction tool and its importance for Bible study?

2. What hints have you found most helpful for seeing the structure of biblical passages?

THE CONSTRUCTION TOOL

3. Define *chiasm* in your own words, as if you were explaining this concept to someone who had never heard of it before.

Respond to the following questions in more depth:

1. How would you describe the shape of Genesis 11:1–9? Think especially about the beginning and ending, the middle, and the verses that mirror each other (such as verses 3 and 7). Are you seeing any kind of structure there?

2. What is right at the center of the chiasm? What, then, might be the emphasis of the text?

CHAPTER 5

_____

_____

1 Samuel 22

Review pages 76–77 in *Understanding God's Word*

First Samuel 22 places David and Saul side by side in this narrative section of Scripture. The story is structured so that it jumps back and forth between the two men, drastically contrasting their character and behavior toward those around them.

Answer the following questions briefly:

1. What happens at the beginning of this passage, verses 1–5? What happens in the longer middle section, verses 6–19? What happens in the final section, verses 20–23?

_____

_____

_____

_____

2. As you use the construction tool in narrative portions of Scripture, what hints might you look for to get an idea of the biblical author's structure and emphasis?

_____

_____

_____

_____

Respond to the following questions in more depth:

THE CONSTRUCTION TOOL

1. How does this structure communicate truth about God's anointed king, David, in contrast with the reigning and evil King Saul?

Psalm 51

Review pages 78–79 in *Understanding God's Word*

Psalm 51 is a prayer of confession, and it has a very clear shape. David's confession relates to what he wants God to do, not only in his heart and life but also in the lives and hearts of God's people.

Answer the following questions briefly:

1. Have you ever been confronted by your sin in a very clear way? How did you respond?

2. How would you define repentance? What would you identify as some steps that lead to repentance? In Psalm 51, what steps toward repentance does David take that might sometimes be missing in our response to our sin?

CHAPTER 5

Respond to the following questions in more depth:

1. If you could divide this psalm into four parts, what would they be? Why would you make the breaks in the places that you chose?

2. If the four parts of this psalm can be seen as different steps of repentance that David takes, how would you summarize each of those steps?

⬦ RECAP

The construction tool can help you find the structure (the shape or organization) of every biblical passage you study. This structure is the author's outline, and it is almost always the key to finding the author's emphasis and main point. Finding that point of emphasis can help protect you against focusing on the wrong things in a Bible passage or missing the correct application.

THE CONSTRUCTION TOOL

⏷ SO WHAT?

As you conclude this chapter, jot down brief answers to the following application questions:

1. In your opinion, what is the most important benefit for Bible study that the construction tool provides? Why is it a valuable tool for interpretation and application?

2. What hints that you have learned about seem most helpful for identifying the structure of passages from the Bible? As you have applied the construction tool, have you discovered other structural hints that you would identify and add?

Respond to the following questions in more depth:

1. It's obviously dangerous to abuse Scripture and teach the opposite of what a particular passage teaches. But why is it also dangerous to miss the main point (or the main emphasis of the biblical author) of a given biblical text? How can this error lead us down wrong paths in both interpretation and application?

65

CHAPTER 5

Chapter 6

THE CLARITY TOOL

Christians believe that the Bible is God's inspired word, given to human beings to help them know and worship him. So when we come to Scripture, we hope to hear God speak. No matter what perspectives or outlooks we bring to the biblical text, that is the goal—if we are serious about meeting God and knowing him through his revelation in the Bible. The clarity tool can help us do this.

UNDERSTANDING THIS TOOL

Review pages 82–84 in *Understanding God's Word*

We all bring a unique set of perspectives, backgrounds, and mindsets to our study of the Bible. Utilizing the clarity tool well helps us resist the tendency to read our own perspectives into the Bible instead of allowing the Bible to rule over our outlooks and speak for itself.

Answer the following questions briefly:

1. List the elements of your life and upbringing that make up your general perspective on the world and on your study of the Bible. How were you raised? Where do you live? What kind of family do you come from? What are your interests? What books have you read? All of these things contribute to your general outlook on life.

CHAPTER 6

2. Think about ways that some people might be in danger of letting their perspectives dominate the way they read, study, interpret, and apply the Bible. Why is it dangerous to read our own perspectives into the Bible?

Respond to the following question in more depth:

1. What are some ways that you can make sure that your general outlook on life does not dominate the way you interpret and apply the Bible? In other words, how can you make sure that the Bible itself is speaking with clarity into your life?

PROBLEMS AVOIDED WITH THIS TOOL

Review pages 84–85 in *Understanding God's Word*

When we utilize this tool effectively, we guard against importing our own ideas, perspectives, and motives into the Bible, making it say what we want it to say. It also can help us resist the temptation to twist, mold, and change Scripture to accomplish our purposes rather than God's.

THE CLARITY TOOL

Answer the following questions briefly:

1. Describe, in general, the way your perspective might naturally lead you to view the Bible. Do you tend to be more conservative? Do you tend to read the Old Testament more than the New Testament? Do you like to talk about grace more than obedience and holiness? Discuss one or two general tendencies you might have with regard to the Bible, given your perspective.

2. Why is it valuable to identify the perspective from which you approach the Bible? How does it help to understand this right at the beginning?

3. Can you think of examples of people teaching a right concept or a good idea from the wrong text? Why might this be helpful in the short term but do damage to the way we approach the Bible?

Respond to the following question in more depth:

69

CHAPTER 6

1. Give an example of a time when you saw or heard about someone who tried to make the Bible fit with his or her own agenda rather than submitting to the truth of what the text was teaching. If you cannot think of such an example, describe a time when you (either accidentally or intentionally) tried to read your own perspective into a text of Scripture. Why was this such a big problem?

BENEFITS RECEIVED WITH THIS TOOL

Review pages 85–87 in *Understanding God's Word*

When we apply the clarity tool effectively, we have the privilege of hearing from God through his word just as he intends. We allow the Bible to rule over our motives and perspectives (and often the Bible confronts the frameworks and mindsets that we bring to Bible study).

Answer the following questions briefly:

1. Among the benefits of this tool for Bible study that we discussed in the book, which did you find most compelling?

2. Do you have any remaining questions about the clarity tool? If so, list them below. In addition to reading the *Understanding God's Word* book, consider taking these

questions to a trusted pastor or ministry leader who can provide you with additional resources for Bible interpretation and application.

Respond to the following question in more depth:

1. Why is it so important to get God's word right as we interpret it, apply it, and teach it to others? What is at stake?

APPLYING THIS TOOL

Let's now see how the clarity tool can help us correctly interpret several passages.

Mark 4:35–41

Review pages 87–89 in *Understanding God's Word*

When we bring our own motives and perspectives to our study of Mark 4:35–41, we can force the passage to be about comfort and help in time of trouble. The passage, though, is not actually about that, for at the end of the passage the disciples are not comforted but troubled—actually terrified—by the person of Jesus Christ.

Answer the following questions briefly:

CHAPTER 6

1. Look at the text again, but leave out the comfort perspective. What is this passage really teaching? What is the main point? Is it about comfort or something else?

2. How can even good perspectives sometimes distract from the main point of a passage in the Bible? Why is it important to leave even good agendas at the door when we come to study God's word?

Respond to the following question in more depth:

1. Read this text and write about it as if you were coming to it with a *comfort* perspective. That is, write as if you know someone who is having many struggles in life, and you want to use this passage to give him or her comfort. How would you apply this passage to his or her life if that perspective were ruling your interpretation?

THE CLARITY TOOL

Revelation 3:20

Review pages 89–91 in *Understanding God's Word*

Many people have sought to interpret Revelation 3:20 from an *evangelistic-witness* perspective—but doing that requires making the text say something that it's not actually about. A careful study of the text reveals the original meaning and intent of the biblical author (and Jesus, who speaks the words).

Answer the following question briefly:

1. Having an evangelistic perspective (which can motivate us to use specific verses in evangelistic conversations) is good. Yet Christians must be careful to use God's word in the right way—as God intends. What dangers might we avoid by being careful not to use biblical passages without clearly understanding their meaning?

Respond to the following questions in more depth:

1. Adopt an evangelistic perspective and let it rule over your interpretation and application of Revelation 3:20. From that perspective, what is Jesus's tone? Who is his audience?

CHAPTER 6

2. Now let the text rule, and consider Revelation 3:14–22, not just verse 20. Now what is Jesus's tone? Who is his audience?

Romans 8:31–39

Review pages 91–93 in *Understanding God's Word*

A *health-and-wealth* perspective can interpret Romans 8:31–39 as a promise of great material blessing for Christians on earth. But allowing the text to speak for itself (using the clarity tool) helps us see a different message that this passage teaches.

Answer the following questions briefly:

1. Have you ever been exposed to the teaching that faith in Jesus should lead to material prosperity, victory, or wealth? If so, where? Why might this kind of teaching be extremely dangerous and damaging to Christians?

2. How do the life, suffering, and death of Jesus Christ prove to us that this teaching is false?

THE CLARITY TOOL

Respond to the following questions in more depth:

1. Imagine bringing a health-and-wealth perspective to this passage. How might you teach it? What promises might you claim from this passage if you are concerned with getting wealthy and enjoying prosperity?

2. What in this passage (and perhaps in the surrounding verses) proves that this is not a passage promising wealth, success, and comfort for all who follow Jesus Christ?

1 Samuel 17

Review pages 93–95 in *Understanding God's Word*

When we identify ourselves with David in 1 Samuel 17, we can force this passage to serve as a motivating example for our own achievement and accomplishment. However, the

CHAPTER 6

passage itself reminds us that David serves as God's anointed and representative warrior king who does battle on behalf of helpless and terrified people.

Answer the following questions briefly:

1. Are you finding the clarity tool to be helpful to you in your study of the Bible? What are some correctives that it has offered to you? Has it helped you identify perspectives and outlooks that you are sometimes tempted to bring to the Bible?

2. How is the clarity tool related to an attitude of humility when it comes to God's word? Why must humility always accompany the use of this tool in Bible study?

Respond to the following questions in more depth as you interact with 1 Samuel 17:

1. Adopt an *individual-motivation* perspective on this passage. In other words, imagine that you are going to use 1 Samuel 17 to motivate yourself or some other individual to action, courage, or accomplishment. How would you apply this passage? What would be your main point? With whom would you identify in the story?

THE CLARITY TOOL

2. Now put the clarity tool to work. What in the text tells you that an individual-motivation perspective is problematic here? With whom should we actually identify in the story?

2 Corinthians 9:6–15

Review pages 95–97 in *Understanding God's Word*

If you were to come to 2 Corinthians 9:6–15 with a *giving-to-the-church* perspective, you might use it to teach about tithing—that is, supporting your local congregation. But when we allow the text itself to speak, we find that the focus is on generous giving to Christians in need in other parts of the world.

Answer the following question briefly:

1. If you were a pastor or church leader whose church needed money to support its programs, its staff, and the care of its building, what are some ways that you might be tempted to use the Bible to help encourage your people to give money to the church?

CHAPTER 6

Respond to the following questions in more depth:

1. If you brought a giving-to-the-church perspective to this passage, what would be the main point and main application?

2. What in the context of the chapter tells us that this passage actually is not about giving to one's local church? What is this passage really about?

Colossians 4:2–6

Review pages 97–98 in *Understanding God's Word*

Colossians 4:2–6 can be used (with good intentions) to encourage Christians to share the gospel in their workplaces. The text itself, though, is a call to prayer for Paul and for the growth and spread of the apostolic gospel—and it must be understood first in this way.

Answer the following questions briefly:

THE CLARITY TOOL

1. Why are Christians called to bear witness to the gospel of Jesus Christ? Why is doing this sometimes hard—and confusing—for people in the context of their jobs and professional lives?

2. How should we be praying about the growth of the gospel in our world? Who should we be praying for as we think about gospel work and ministry?

Respond to the following questions in more depth:

1. Bring a *sharing-the-gospel-at-work* perspective to this text. Imagine that you are letting that perspective rule over the text as you call a group of professionals to share Jesus in their offices. How would you interpret and apply this text?

CHAPTER 6

2. Now apply the clarity tool to this text. What is Paul's first focus in these verses? How does he make a call to gospel witness to the church members in the city of Colossae?

RECAP

The clarity tool is important for the right interpretation and application of Scripture. The sad reality is that many people import their own perspectives into Bible study and allow them to rule over God's word as they interpret and apply it. The clarity tool reminds us that the Bible itself must rule; our goal is to sit under its authority and do everything we can to let it speak clearly and powerfully to our lives.

SO WHAT?

As you conclude this chapter, jot down brief answers to the following application questions:

1. Discuss the ways that the clarity tool will be especially beneficial for you in your own study.

2. Give some examples of ways that you have seen people twist or use Scripture to fit their own perspectives or agendas. How are you able to identify this practice more clearly after working through this chapter?

Respond to the following questions in more depth:

1. Define and explain the clarity tool as if you were introducing it to someone who had never heard of it and is just beginning to study the Bible. How would you summarize it? What is the main principle behind it? What dangers does it help Bible students avoid, and what are its main benefits?

Chapter 7

THE CROSS TOOL

Far too often, Bible students seek to understand and apply passages of Scripture without considering them in light of the death and resurrection of Jesus Christ—the message of the gospel. To help us guard against making this mistake in our own study of the Bible, we have a useful sixth tool that we can add to our hermeneutical tool belts—the cross tool.

UNDERSTANDING THIS TOOL

Review pages 102–3 in *Understanding God's Word*

The cross tool reminds us that since the person and work of Jesus Christ is the true central climax of God's word, every part of the Bible must be interpreted and applied with reference to Jesus and his gospel.

Answer the following questions briefly:

1. Other than the gospel, what are some areas of focus that people have in the study of the Bible?

CHAPTER 7

2. Why do we often tend to miss the gospel when we study the Bible? Why do we miss it especially often when we are studying Old Testament passages?

3. Can you think of any passages in the Bible that remind us that the gospel should be central in our study of every part of God's word?

Respond to the following question in more depth:

1. Give your own definition of the gospel as you understand it currently. Then give some examples of how different parts of the Bible point to this gospel clearly. If you can, give at least one example from the Old Testament.

THE CROSS TOOL

PROBLEMS AVOIDED WITH THIS TOOL

Review pages 103–5 in *Understanding God's Word*

Using the cross tool effectively in our study of the Bible protects us from purely moralistic and legalistic interpretations—especially of Old Testament passages—and the guilt such interpretations can lead to. It also guards us against a wrong view of the Bible, one that misses Jesus, whose person and work is the climax of the entire story of redemption.

Answer the following questions briefly:

1. Is the concept of the gospel's centrality in every part of the Bible new to you? If so, do you feel that you are understanding it well? If it is not new to you, where did you learn this concept and how has it helped you?

2. What might people miss in Bible study if they ignore the cross of Jesus?

Respond to the following question in more depth:

1. Select a passage from the Old Testament and write about how it might be interpreted without the use of the cross tool. In other words, do not bring the gospel into the process of trying to summarize the point of this passage.

CHAPTER 7

BENEFITS RECEIVED WITH THIS TOOL

Review pages 105–6 in *Understanding God's Word*

The cross tool helps us read the Bible as one story and helps us read it the way Jesus did—by relating both the Old Testament and the New Testament to his central work of salvation for sinners. This way of reading helps us find grace.

Answer the following questions briefly:

1. Other than those mentioned above, what are some benefits of using this tool well that you might identify?

2. What do you still not understand about the cross tool? Why is it sometimes confusing to try to get to the gospel from Old Testament passages?

Respond to the following question in more depth:

1. How does the cross tool relate to the doctrine of inspiration (that God "breathed out" the words of Scripture by inspiring the men who wrote it; 2 Tim. 3:16)? Explain

the connection between the centrality of the gospel in the Bible and God as the one who put together this one big story of his salvation in the world.

APPLYING THIS TOOL

Review pages 106–8 in *Understanding God's Word*

The Old Testament points to Christ in many different ways—through types, patterns and themes, depictions of our need of salvation, and prophecies and promises that anticipated his saving work for God's people.

Answer the following questions briefly:

1. From what you already know about the Old Testament, discuss some paths to the gospel that you might find there. How does the Old Testament point us to Jesus's death for sins and his resurrection from the dead?

2. What challenges have you experienced in your study of the Old Testament? What makes it difficult to use the cross tool as you study passages from Genesis, Judges, or 2 Samuel?

CHAPTER 7

Respond to the following question in more depth:

1. Can you think of some obvious passages or pictures from the Old Testament that seem to point ahead to Jesus and his life, death, and resurrection? Discuss how they do this.

Let's now see how the cross tool can help us correctly interpret several passages.

Joshua 5:13–15

Review pages 108–9 in *Understanding God's Word*

Without the cross tool, Joshua 5:13–15 can be a good reminder about leadership, humility, and being led by God. By using the cross tool, however, we also see how this passage points us forward to Jesus Christ, the greater Joshua before whom we all must bow in worship.

Answer the following questions briefly:

1. What do you already know about Joshua? Who was he, and what did he help God's people accomplish?

THE CROSS TOOL

2. What are some challenges that you see in getting to the gospel from the Old Testament? How might some of these challenges come up as you study a book like Joshua?

Respond to the following questions in more depth:

1. If you do not use the cross tool in your study of Joshua 5:13–15, what main point and main application are you likely to come away with?

2. If you do use the cross tool in your study of this passage, how does it change the way you interpret and apply it?

CHAPTER 7

Judges 2:6–15

Review pages 109–10 in *Understanding God's Word*

Judges 2:6–15 shows the sin of God's people and their need for a king. The cross tool reminds us to take these truths even further by looking ahead to the only King who can rule over sinful people by saving them perfectly and eternally.

Answer the following questions briefly:

1. What glaring needs for the people of God does this passage identify? What are their successes and failures? What seems incomplete in this passage?

2. When you think about the book of Judges, what pictures or themes come to mind? How do you think that the entire book of Judges might point us to Jesus?

Respond to the following questions in more depth:

1. If you do not use the cross tool in your study of Judges 2:6–15, where must your interpretation and application stop? Where do you land as you summarize the main point?

THE CROSS TOOL

2. When you do put the cross tool to work in this passage, how does your perspective change? What do you see this passage revealing to us?

1 Samuel 13:1–14

Review pages 110–13 in *Understanding God's Word*

First Samuel 13:1–14, which shows us the failure of King Saul, can be used as simply a call to obedience. When we use the cross tool, however, we also see that this passage gives us a hint—by showing us Saul's failure—of a greater King and high priest who was still to come.

Answer the following questions briefly:

1. Discuss how the cross tool helps us focus on Jesus—God's Son—as the central character in the Bible. Why is this so important?

CHAPTER 7

2. Why is 1 Samuel 13:1–14 a good example of an Old Testament passage that could be interpreted and applied in a simply moralistic way—without mentioning Jesus at all?

Respond to the following questions in more depth:

1. What does Saul try to do in this passage? What two roles is he trying to fulfill? Why is Saul rejected—by God and by Samuel—as a result of his actions?

2. When we put the cross tool to work in this passage, in what ways can we see that it points us to Jesus and the gospel?

THE CROSS TOOL

1 Kings 10:1–13

Review pages 113–14 in *Understanding God's Word*

King Solomon's failure and downward slide remind us that even at the height of the kingdom of Israel, God's people were called to anticipate a greater Son of David who would rule in glory and without sin.

Answer the following questions briefly:

1. You saw how a negative example (King Saul) can point to Jesus. While King Solomon demonstrates failure as well (especially later in his reign), how can positive pictures from his reign point us to the perfect reign of King Jesus?

2. Explain how each part of God's promise to Abraham is being fulfilled in this passage.

Respond to the following questions in more depth:

1. If we do not put the cross tool to work in this passage, how will we interpret and apply it? If we do use the cross tool, how does this passage point us to the gospel?

CHAPTER 7

Ezra 3

Review pages 114–15 in *Understanding God's Word*

Ezra 3, without the cross tool, becomes a passage celebrating the accomplishment of a group of people as they return to the land of promise and rebuild. However, the cross tool helps us make sense of the weeping of the old men and points us ahead to a greater temple.

Answer the following questions briefly:

1. What is it about the cross tool that makes your interpretation and application of the Bible deeper and more powerful? Why is gospel-centered application better than moralism?

2. As you think about the historical situation of Ezra (God's people returning to the land and rebuilding the temple), what paths to the gospel might you expect to find in this book?

Respond to the following questions in more depth:

THE CROSS TOOL

1. If you do not put the cross tool to work in the study of this passage, what will you see as its main point and main application?

2. How is verse 12 absolutely crucial to a gospel-centered interpretation and application of this passage? How does the cross tool help you read that verse and apply it accurately?

⬦ RECAP

Using the cross tool in your study and application of biblical passages helps you see the gospel as the center of the Bible. Therefore, this perspective makes an impact on your study of every page of it. This is the way Jesus himself reads the Bible. After he rose from the dead, he took time to show his disciples that his life, death, and resurrection fulfill all of the Law, the Prophets, and the Psalms (Luke 24:44–47). So when we put the cross tool to work, we are trying to read and study the Bible the way that Jesus did.

CHAPTER 7

▼ SO WHAT?

As you conclude this chapter, jot down brief answers to the following application questions:

1. In your opinion, what is the most important benefit that the cross tool provides for the study of the Bible? What mistakes does it protect you from as you study? How does it make application more powerful?

2. How has your perspective on the Old Testament changed during this chapter? Discuss any specific ways that you have seen how passages from the Old Testament point forward powerfully to the work of Jesus.

Respond to the following question in more depth:

1. Define the cross tool as if you are explaining it to someone who has never heard of it. Explain how it is based on an understanding of the climax of the Bible. Give a couple of examples of how you might put it to work in your study of the Old Testament.

THE CROSS TOOL

Available from the Theology Basics Series

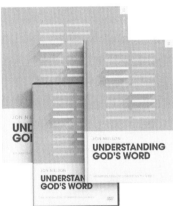

The Theology Basics series is a collection of books, workbooks, and videos designed to provide an accessible introduction to the study of biblical truth—systematic theology, biblical theology, and biblical interpretation.

For more information, visit **crossway.org**.